Perthshire & Kinross-shire's Lost Railways

by
Gordon Stansfield

0-4-4T no. 55200 near Grandtully on the Aberfeldy–Ballinluig line, May 1959.

THE PUBLISHERS REGRET THAT THEY CANNOT SUPPLY
COPIES OF ANY PICTURES FEATURED IN THIS BOOK.

ACKNOWLEDGEMENTS
The publishers wish to thank the following for permission to reproduce
photographs in this book: Hugh Brodie for the front and back covers, the
inside back cover and pages 2, 4, 5, 8, 9, 12, 16, 17, 27, 32, 35–42 and 44–48;
W.A.C. Smith for pages 3, 6, 14, 15, 18–22, 24–26, 29 and 34; Neville Stead and
D. Butterfield for page 1; and Neville Stead and P.B. Booth for page 33.

King Edward VII at Blairgowrie Station.

The King's Visit to Blairgowrie, September 1908
His Majesty at Station

INTRODUCTION

At the turn of the twentieth century when Britain's railways were at their peak, the counties of Perth and Kinross could boast a substantial rail network consisting of one hundred and sixteen stations. Today that number has been reduced to just eleven.

When the railways first reached Perthshire in 1847 (and Kinross-shire shortly afterwards) they brought new business opportunities and financial benefits to many towns and villages, ranging from tourism to cheap transport of agricultural produce.

In the early days most lines were built with local support before being amalgamated into the larger railway companies of the day. Perth, for example, became a very important railway location served by the Caledonian, North British and Highland railway companies and its station was the centre of numerous overnight trains from the south, all of which converged just before dawn before heading northwards to Inverness and Aberdeen.

The counties also had many branch lines which linked into the main lines. Even as late as 1906 new railways were still being built, such as the one to Bankfoot. Every town and village wanted its own railway and most achieved this. Places such as Aberfeldy, Callander, Crieff, Alyth, Comrie, Balquhidder, Kinross and Killin all had their railways.

Most of the lines ran through spectacular countryside such as the Callander and Oban route which went through Glen Ogle. The engineers of these lines were remarkable and many of their structures can still be seen today, decades after closure, such as the curved viaduct near Lochearnhead. For years special sightseeing trains operated, allowing many city folks to experience the joy of the countryside for the very first time at a price they could afford.

The very nature of railway operations resulted in oddities such as the station of Killin Junction which was only accessible by rail. Trains stopped once a week near remote railway workers' cottages so that families could go shopping. Even into the early 1960s there was a school train, consisting of just one coach, which ran from Killin to Callander.

For many of today's generation whose transport is the car, the experience of rural rail travel is something they will never know. But for those who enjoyed it in its heyday, it is hoped that this book will rekindle many fond memories.

Highlandman Station, looking towards Muthill, August 1955.

Aberfeldy — Ballinluig (Aberfeldy Junction)

Passenger service withdrawn	3 May 1965	*Stations closed*	*Date*
Distance	8.75 miles	Aberfeldy	3 May 1965
Company	Highland	Grandtully	3 May 1965
		Balnaguard	3 May 1965

Grandtully Station.

This line was authorised in 1861 as a branch of the Highland Railway's Inverness to Perth line. It was opened on 3 July 1865 with only one intermediate station at Grandtully. On 2 December 1935 the London, Midland & Scottish Railway Company opened a halt at Balnaguard. There were no crossing loops at any of the intermediate stations. In the winter of 1963–64 the line operated five return journeys Monday to Friday with six on Saturdays. This level of service compared favourably with that in 1922 when there were six return journeys Monday to Saturday. Like most of the other Highland lines a Sunday service never operated. In the last months before closure the line boasted a one-coach train hauled by a diesel locomotive – a very expensive service to provide. Aberfeldy and Grandtully had freight facilities and these were withdrawn on 25 January 1965. Train services serving Ballinluig on the Perth to Inverness line were also withdrawn on 3 May 1965.

Aberfoyle — Kirkintilloch *

Passenger service withdrawn	1 October 1951	*Stations closed*		*Date*
Distance	26.25 miles	Aberfoyle		1 October 1951
Company	North British	Gartmore		2 January 1950

Aberfoyle Station.

Known as the Blane Valley Railway, this line was opened in several stages. The first part reached Kirkintilloch and Lennoxtown after leaving the main Edinburgh to Glasgow route at Lenzie Junction. The section from Lennoxtown to Dumgoyne was opened in July 1867 and the remainder to Gartness and from Buchlyvie to Aberfoyle opened in October 1882. Through trains from Glasgow Queen Street High Level Station made up the traffic on the line for most of its life. In the years before closure many trains terminated at Blanefield where a one-coach train operated to and from Aberfoyle. By 1949 the service had been reduced to such an extent that Aberfoyle had just two arrivals and departures on weekdays, and three on Saturdays. In 1955 Gartmore Station, by then closed, was used as a set for the Alastair Sim film *Geordie*.

* Closed stations on this line in Stirlingshire were Buchlyvie, Balfron, Killearn, Dumgoyne, Blanefield, Strathblane, Campsie Glen, Lennoxtown (Blane Valley), Lennoxtown and Milton of Campsie.

Alyth — Alyth Junction (Alyth Branch Junction)

Passenger service withdrawn	2 July 1951	*Stations closed*	*Date*
Distance	5 miles	Alyth	2 July 1951
Company	Caledonian	Pitcrocknie Siding *	2 July 1951
		Jordanstone	2 July 1951
		Meigle **	2 July 1951

A Caledonian Jumbo 0-6-0, no. 57441, calling at Meigle with a railtour special, June 1960.

This was one of several branch lines which the Caledonian built between Stanley and Kinnaber Junctions as offshoots from its main line which served Perth and Aberdeen. Opened on 12 August 1861, the line from Alyth Junction Station to the small town of Alyth was fairly easy to construct. Pitcrocknie Siding was situated about a mile from Alyth and trains only stopped if there were passengers on the platform or to set down golfers for access to the nearby golf course. Trains ran from Alyth to Dundee, with the journey for this 23 mile trip taking about an hour and twenty-five minutes for a train stopping at all stations and an hour for a semi-fast service. At Alyth Junction Station connections could be made for numerous locations as express trains between Aberdeen and Glasgow stopped there. In the days when the London Midland & Scottish Railway Company operated services to Alyth there were about nine departures on weekdays with two extra on Saturdays. One year after nationalisation the level of services had become very limited indeed, and in 1949 there were only two arrivals and two departures at Alyth. Although Pitcrocknie Siding was removed from the public timetable following nationalisation in 1948 it was not officially closed and still picked up or set down passengers. Freight services to Alyth and Meigle continued until January 1965, while those to Pitcrocknie Siding were withdrawn in August 1955. Freight services to Jordanstone ceased in September 1964.

* Known as Pitcrocknie Platform until 28 October 1940.

** Known as Fullarton until 1 November 1876.

Alyth West Junction — Newtyle

Passenger service withdrawn	10 January 1955	*Distance*	2 miles
		Company	Caledonian

This line was a spur off the Caledonian's main line between Stanley Junction and Kinnaber Junction. It left the main line to the west of Alyth Junction and ran to Newtyle Station, thereby allowing services to run to and from Dundee. The services which used the spur generally began at Blairgowrie and that branch closed on the same date. As there were no stations on this line the need for closure procedures was minimal. For most of its life there were about five return workings daily Monday to Saturday.

Balquhidder (Balquhidder Junction) — Comrie

Passenger service withdrawn	1 October 1951
Distance	15.25 miles
Company	Caledonian

Stations closed	*Date*
Lochearnhead	1 October 1951
St Fillans	1 October 1951
Dalchonzie Halt	1 October 1951

Lochearnhead Station.

St Fillans Station.

The line from Balquhidder to Comrie continued onwards to Crieff where it diverged for either Gleneagles or Perth. At Balquhidder connections were available on the Callander and Oban line to Oban in the west and Callander and Stirling in the south. The line to Crieff from Perth was built by the Perth, Almond Valley & Methven Railway but the extension west to Comrie and Balquhidder was built by the Crieff & Methven Junction Railway. It was opened in several stages: the Comrie to St Fillans stretch on 1 October 1901; St Fillans to Lochearnhead on 1 July 1904; and Lochearnhead to Balquhidder on 1 May 1905. Lochearnhead and St Fillans had freight facilities whilst Dalchonzie Halt was just a platform where trains stopped on request. Balquhidder Station on the Callander and Oban line was originally called Lochearnhead, even though it was a mile from Lochearnhead village, but when the line from Crieff was opened it had its name changed to Balquhidder. In the 1930s, with the increase in leisure travel, there was a Sunday only service along the line from Dundee to Oban picking up at all stations apart from Dalchonzie Halt. During the summer months evening excursion trains from Glasgow and Edinburgh also used the line. By 1950 the traffic along the route was sparse and both passenger and freight services were withdrawn on 1 October 1951.

Bankfoot — Strathord (Bankfoot Junction)

Passenger service withdrawn	13 April 1931	Station closed	Date
Distance	3 miles	Bankfoot	13 April 1931
Company	Caledonian		

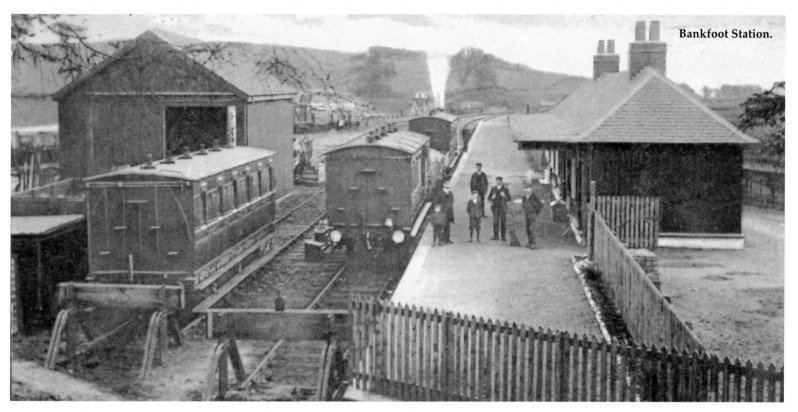

Bankfoot Station.

The three mile branch line from Bankfoot joined the Caledonian main line north of Perth at Strathord Station; this was south of Stanley Junction where the Caledonian and Highland Railway lines diverged allowing passengers to travel to either Aberdeen or Inverness. Built as the Bankfoot Light Railway by the Caledonian, the line opened to passengers on 1 May 1906. Most trains from Bankfoot continued south to Perth which was only 5 miles from Strathord. In 1922 there were seven return journeys Monday to Friday with two more on Saturdays. Patronage was very low although after closure to passengers in 1931 the line remained open until 1964 for potato traffic. Strathord Station also closed on 13 April 1931. When the new A9 road was under construction in the late 1980s part of the old trackbed was incorporated into the highway.

Blairgowrie — Coupar Angus (Blairgowrie Junction)

Passenger service withdrawn	10 January 1955	*Stations closed*	*Date*
Distance	4.75 miles	Blairgowrie	10 January 1955
Company	Caledonian	Rosemount	10 January 1955

Rosemount Station.

The Blairgowrie to Coupar Angus line was one of eleven branches which left the Caledonian main line between Stanley Junction and Kinnaber Junction. Opened in 1855, it lasted a century before losing its passenger service. It was the first branch line to be encountered travelling north from Perth, and crossed the River Isla one-and-a-quarter miles west of Coupar Angus. In winter the Isla sometimes rose to eleven or more feet above its summer level, causing problems for the Caledonian's engineers. The pattern of service along this line permitted trains from Blairgowrie to Coupar Angus to continue eastwards to Ardler where they could head south on the Dundee and Newtyle line to Dundee. The running time on the branch was ten minutes, with most trains stopping at the intermediate halt at Rosemount. Freight services to Blairgowrie lasted until 1965.

Bridge of Earn (Bridge of Earn Junction) — Cowdenbeath (North Junction) *

Passenger service withdrawn	5 January 1970	*Stations closed*	*Date*
Distance	22 miles	Mawcarse	15 June 1964
Company	North British	Milnathort	15 June 1964
		Kinross	20 September 1860
Stations closed	*Date*	Kinross Junction (first)	June 1890
Bridge of Earn (first)	1 February 1892	Kinross Junction	5 January 1970
Bridge of Earn (second)	15 June 1964	Loch Leven	1 September 1921
Abernethy Road	25 July 1848	Blairadam	22 September 1930
Glenfarg	15 June 1964		

* The closed station on this line in Fife was Kelty.

No. 62492 at Bridge of Earn Station, August 1955.

Glenfarg Station.

Different parts of this line were built and owned by different railway companies prior to its acquisition by the North British Railway Company. It was one of several routes considered as a possibility for providing a rail link between Edinburgh and Perth via the Forth Bridge. The North British wanted it to have main line status and consequently it had to be upgraded in many areas in order to cope with this type of traffic. At Kinross Junction Station the Devon Valley line headed westwards towards Dollar and Alloa. This line was closed on 15 June 1964. South of Kinross Junction was Loch Leven, which in the early twentieth century hosted curling competitions when the loch became frozen during the winter months. This necessitated the running of special trains, often at short notice, to carry competitors and spectators. Interest in curling waned after the First World War and Loch Leven Station closed to passengers on 1 September 1921. Through trains to Edinburgh continued to use the line up until closure and were then diverted via the Bridge of Earn to Ladybank line which had been closed in September 1955 but was subsequently reopened to cater for these trains. The only remaining station on the line between 1964 and 1970 was Kinross Junction, which was quickly demolished after closure to make way for the new M90 motorway.

On the line near Glenfarg.

IN GLENFARG

Preserved North British 4-4-0 no. 256, 'Glen Douglas', runs round its train at Mawcarse Station (to go to Auchtermuchty), June 1960. This was a special working for railway enthusiasts.

Black Five no. 44973 at Kinross Junction Station with the 4.20 p.m. train
from Perth to Glasgow (Queen Street), April 1959.

Bridge of Earn (Bridge of Earn Junction) — Ladybank (Ladybank North Junction) *

Passenger service withdrawn	19 September 1955	*Stations closed*	*Date*
Distance	15.25 miles	Abernethy	19 September 1955
Company	North British		

This line was opened on 18 July 1845 by the Scottish Central Railway Company which introduced services between Perth and Edinburgh. With the establishment of the North British service between Edinburgh and Perth via Kinross Junction, the importance of the line diminished. There was a branch from Newburgh to St Fort on the Dundee to Edinburgh east coast main line, and trains using this line often began their journey at Perth and travelled along the Bridge to Earn to Ladybank line as far as Newburgh. There were about five return journeys on the line Monday to Saturday, with all trains starting at Perth. When these were withdrawn in 1955 the line was retained for freight traffic. Despite a severe line blockage in January 1967 at Clatchland Craig Quarry, which could have threatened the line's future, October 1975 saw the reintroduction of passenger traffic when services from Inverness/Perth to Edinburgh were restarted.

* Closed stations on this line in Fife were Newburgh, Lindores, Glenburnie, Collessie.

Callander — Dunblane (Dunblane Junction)

Passenger service withdrawn	1 November 1965	*Stations closed*	*Date*
Distance	11.25 miles	Callander	1 June 1870
Company	Caledonian	Callander Dreadnought	1 November 1965
		Doune	1 November 1965

Callander Station.

Doune Station.

This line formed the easterly section of the Callander and Oban line which ran from Callander via Strathyre, Glen Ogle, Crianlarich and Taynuilt to Oban, a distance of 71 miles. The Callander to Dunblane line was promoted by the Dunblane, Doune and Callander Railway Company and opened to passenger traffic on 1 July 1858. The line from Callander to Oban was opened in stages, with Oban being reached in July 1880. When completed it offered an alternative route from Oban to Edinburgh or Glasgow (the other option was the present route on the West Highland line from Craigendoran to Crianlarich). The Dunblane, Doune & Callander Railway Company was taken over by the Scottish Central Railway Company on 31 July 1865 and by the Caledonian Railway Company the following day. Most services on the line went as far as Oban, but there were additional journeys between Callander and Stirling. There was always an overnight train in each direction between Glasgow and Oban with through coaches from London including sleeping cars. In British Railways days the sleeping cars left Oban at 5.30 p.m. In June 1935 just under four miles of the line was completely realigned between Dunblane and Callander. In the late 1950s British Railways ran the very popular Six Lochs Land Cruise on Sundays using diesel multiple units. At Callander passengers could have Sunday lunch before proceeding north to Killin Junction Station where the train reversed for Killin. The service then returned to Killin Junction and continued to Crianlarich where it joined the West Highland line to return to Glasgow. A reduction in traffic, plus the fact that there was a quicker route to Oban via the West Highland line, resulted in the whole line being scheduled for closure on 1 November 1965. However, only the Callander to Dunblane section officially closed on that date as a landslide in September of the same year resulted in the line being blocked between Callander and Crianlarich and never reopening. Freight services from Callander and Doune stations were withdrawn in June 1965.

Comrie — Gleneagles (Gleneagles Junction)

Passenger service withdrawn	6 July 1964		*Stations closed*	*Date*
Distance	15 miles		Pittenzie Halt	6 July 1964
Company	Caledonian		Highlandman *	6 July 1964
			Strageath Halt	6 July 1964
Stations closed	*Date*		Muthill	6 July 1964
Comrie	6 July 1964		Tullibardine	6 July 1964
Crieff (first)	1 June 1893			
Crieff (second)	6 July 1964		* Closed between January 1917 and February 1919.	

A class 4F 0-6-0, no. 44193, at Comrie, August 1955.

Black Five no. 44721 at Crieff Station with the 12 noon train to Gleneagles, August 1963. The steam locomotive was deputising for a diesel railbus.

The line from Comrie to Gleneagles was constructed by two different railway companies. At Crieff there was a junction with a line going east to Perth and another going south to Gleneagles. The section from Comrie to Crieff was built by the Crieff and Methven Junction Railway and opened to passengers in July 1893, while the line from Crieff to Gleneagles was opened in March 1856 by the Scottish Central Railway. Known as the Crieff Junction Railway, this line took longer to build than envisaged due to difficulties in acquiring land from a local landowner who wanted a private station built for his exclusive use. By the late 1860s the Caledonian had taken over the line and was operating trains between Crieff and Gleneagles. Gleneagles Station is situated on the main line between Stirling and Perth and afforded good connections from Crieff; its famous hotel was originally built to accommodate well-to-do railway customers. Crieff was one of a number of towns in which the Caledonian offered reduced fares to people who bought villas in the area.

A Wickham railbus, no. SC79968, passing Pittenzie Halt on the 2.10 p.m. run from Gleneagles to Creiff, January 1960.

British Railways also tried to stimulate traffic on this line, but in a different manner, by opening new halts at Pittenzie and Strageath in the 1950s. The line saw the use of railbuses, with some journeys being operated by Park Royal four-wheeled vehicles. However, steam lasted right until the end with the usual train comprising one locomotive and two coaches. Some of the stations, including Comrie, Highlandman and Tullibardine, became unstaffed in 1959. Services from Crieff to Perth and Comrie to Balquhidder were withdrawn in October 1951. The final timetable for the line gave departures from Comrie for Gleneagles at 7.45 a.m., 9.40 a.m. and 6.45 p.m. There were an additional seven journeys from Crieff to Gleneagles. Only one service went further afield with the first morning train from Gleneagles to Crieff starting at Stirling. Freight services were withdrawn in November 1964.

Crianlarich Lower (Crianlarich Junction East) — Callander

Passenger service withdrawn	28 September 1965
Distance	30 miles
Company	Caledonian

Stations closed	*Date*
Crianlarich Lower	28 September 1965
Luib	28 September 1965
Glenoglehead Crossing *	December 1916

Stations closed	*Date*
Balquhidder (first) **	1 May 1905
Kingshouse Platform	28 September 1965
Strathyre	28 September 1965

* Known as Killin until 1 April 1886 and then as Glenoglehead until 30 September 1891.

** Known as Lochearnhead until 1 May 1904.

Crianlarich Lower Station, looking west, July 1957.

A preserved Caledonian 4-2-2, no. 123, at Luib in the aftermath of a blizzard with a 'Scottish Rambler' railtour from Glasgow, April 1963.

The line from Crianlarich to Callander formed part of the easterly section of the route from Oban to Stirling which was known as the Callander and Oban line. Today all that remains is the section from Oban to Crianlarich. Opened in sections, this line was very spectacular with through trains from Glasgow and Edinburgh often being double-headed. The line had two branches. At Killin Junction Station, which was inaccessible by road, there was a branch line to Killin and Loch Tay; the other branch was the route from Balquhidder to Comrie, Crieff and onwards to Perth. Balquhidder Station became quite an important place and at one time had an engine shed, two signal boxes and a station whose buildings were used for non-railway purposes such as a polling station and a local council chamber.

Strathyre Station.

However, the line to Perth closed in 1951 and it was in the ensuing years that this once-busy through route to Oban began to decline. Trains to Oban could travel via the West Highland line to Crianlarich from Glasgow, and traffic beyond Callander was minimal. Fate took a hand in closing the line. The official closure date had been fixed as 1 November 1965, but a landslide at Glenoglehead resulted in services ceasing from September 1965. Today a section of the former Callander and Oban line forms part of a walkway from Callander to Strathyre and on to Glenoglehead.

Creiff — Perth (Almond Valley Junction)

Passenger service withdrawn	1 October 1951	*Stations closed*	*Date*
Distance	16 miles	Madderty	1 October 1951
Company	Caledonian	Balgowan	1 October 1951
		Methven Junction	1 October 1951
Stations closed	*Date*	Tibbermuir **	1 October 1951
Innerpeffray *	1 October 1951	Almondbank	1 October 1951
Abercairny	1 October 1951	Ruthven Road ***	1 October 1951

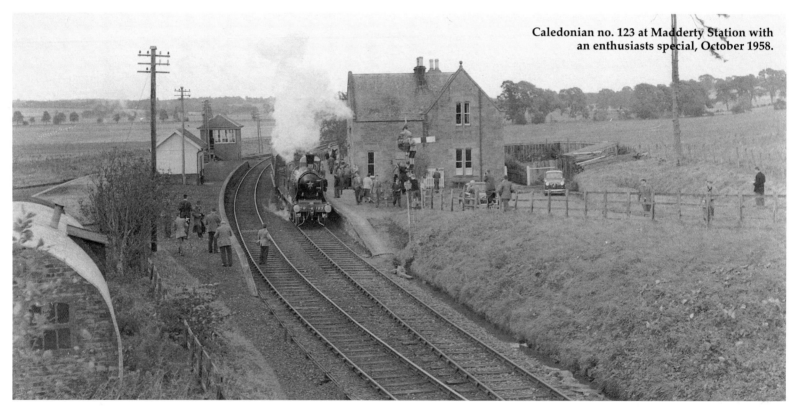

Caledonian no. 123 at Madderty Station with an enthusiasts special, October 1958.

* Closed between January 1917 and June 1919.

** Known as Tibbermuir Crossing until December 1938.
*** Known as Ruthven Road Crossing until December 1935.

Caledonian no. 123 at isolated Methven Junction Station, October 1958.

The line from Perth to Crieff extended further westwards towards Balquhidder where it joined the line from Stirling to Oban. Known as the Perth, Almond Valley & Methven Railway, it reached Crieff in May 1866. At Methven Junction there was a short branch line to Methven and at Crieff the line continued to Gleneagles. There were no large towns along the route but there were a few wayside stations. For many years Methven Junction Station failed to be mentioned in timetables and along with Ruthven Road had no freight facilities. There were about four trains in each direction daily, two of which went on to Balquhidder. A Sentinel railcar operated from Perth to Methven Junction and on to Methven for many years. Freight services along the line lasted until the mid-1960s.

Preserved NBR 4-4-0 no. 256, 'Glen Douglas', at the former station
at Tibbermuir with a 'Scottish Rambler' railtour, April 1962.

Inchture Village — Inchture (Inchture Junction)

Passenger service withdrawn	1 January 1917	*Stations closed*	*Date*
Distance	1.5 miles	Inchture Village	1 January 1917
Company	Caledonian		

Inchture Station.

Opened in 1848, this short branch was not really a railway but a horse-drawn tramway. The line between Inchture Village and Inchture was fairly level, thus making the service easy to operate. Services ran to Inchture Station which was on the Perth to Dundee line. Before closure in 1917 there were about six return workings on weekdays.

Killin — Killin Junction

Passenger service withdrawn	28 September 1965	*Stations closed*	*Date*
Distance	4 miles	Killin	28 September 1965
Company	Killin Railway	Killin Junction	28 September 1965

Killin Junction Station.

The branch line from Killin Junction to Killin originally continued on to Loch Tay, but this section of the line lost its passenger service on 1 September 1939 when steamer services on the loch were withdrawn between Loch Tay Pier and Kenmore. As the engine shed for the line was based at Loch Tay, engines continued to use this stretch of line. Opened for passenger traffic on 1 April 1886, the line remained independent although it was worked by the Caledonian Railway Company until the main grouping in 1923. The traction and rolling stock consisted of one engine and coach. Connections were available to Oban and Callander from Killin Junction Station. The pattern of service remained unchanged into British Railways days and in 1964, the year prior to closure, there were four departures on weekdays. In 1949 there had been five whilst in 1926 there had been eight with four of these continuing to and from Loch Tay. Rail specials using newly-introduced diesel multiple units visited the line in the early 1960s on what was known as the Six Lochs Land Cruise. The withdrawal of passenger services was brought forward from 1 November to 28 September by the landslide at Glenoglehead.

Kinross Junction — Alloa (East Junction) *

Passenger service withdrawn	15 June 1964	*Station closed*	*Date*
Distance	17 miles	Glenfoot	December 1851
Company	North British	Rumbling Bridge (first)	1 October 1868
		Rumbling Bridge (second)	15 June 1964

Station closed	*Date*
Balado	15 June 1964
Crook of Devon	15 June 1964

* Closed stations on this line that were in Clackmannanshire were Dollar, Tillicoultry and Sauchie.

Known as the Devon Valley line, this cross-country route linked the Perth to Cowdenbeath line at Kinross Junction with the Dunfermline to Stirling line at Alloa. Opened along its entire length in 1871, the line was very difficult to construct. When completed there were sixteen bridges in the section between Dollar and Rumbling Bridge, including two viaducts. Severe gradients in some sections of the route caused further problems, and at Rumbling Bridge the North British engineer decided that the line gave too steep a descent into Dollar. It subsequently had to be altered, resulting in the closure of the first Rumbling Bridge Station. In the latter years of its operation there was only one train in each direction which traversed the whole of the line.

Loch Tay — Killin

Passenger service withdrawn	9 September 1939	*Stations closed*	*Date*
Distance	1 mile	Loch Tay	9 September 1939
Company	Caledonian		

Loch Tay is fourteen and a half miles long and some trains from Killin Junction continued beyond Killin to Loch Tay Station in order to connect with steamer sailings. In the mid-1920s there were four return journeys to and from Loch Tay and three steamer journeys between Loch Tay (also known as Killin Pier) and Kenmore, with a motor bus connection to Aberfeldy. After the summer of 1939 the steamer service was withdrawn, resulting in the rail passenger service suffering the same fate, although the line stayed in use as its locomotive was stabled at the engine shed at Loch Tay. Freight traffic also used the line in connection with a hydroelectric scheme for a period in the 1950s.

The long-closed Loch Tay Station, June 1948.

Methven — Methven Junction

Passenger service withdrawn	27 September 1937	*Station closed*	*Date*
Distance	1.25 miles	Methven	27 September 1937
Company	Caledonian		

Methven Station.

This branch left the Perth to Crieff line at Methven Junction. Following the creation of a junction one mile short of Methven, which allowed through services to Crieff to begin in May 1866, the village found itself in the position of not being on a through route between Perth and Crieff but instead on the stub of a branch line. However, as the junction station by its very location did not allow for trains from Methven to call there, services were provided to and from Perth up until closure. In 1927 the London, Midland & Scottish Railway Company introduced a steam rail bus on the route from Perth to Methven which could carry about seventy passengers when pressed. There were about four arrivals and departures on weekdays with an additional journey on Saturdays. The journey time was about half an hour. After the withdrawal of passenger services, specials continued to visit the line which remained open for freight traffic until January 1965. One was entitled 'Scottish Rambler' and visited the line in June 1960. At that time, 23 years after closure, the station buildings were still in fairly good condition.

Newtyle (Nethermill Junction) — Meigle Junction

Passenger service withdrawn	1 August 1861	*Stations closed*	*Date*
Distance	1.75 miles	Meigle Junction	1 August 1861
Company	Scottish Midland Joint		

This line was built to allow passengers to travel from Dundee to Forfar and Kirriemuir. Opened in 1838, it became obsolete when the line from Newtyle was extended northwards to a station at Alyth Junction which was on the Stanley to Craigo main line and afforded better connections to Forfar and Kirriemuir.

The railway bridge over the River Isla, near Coupar Angus.

Stanley (Stanley Junction) — Craigo (Kinnaber Junction) *

Passenger service withdrawn	4 September 1967	*Stations closed*	*Date*
Distance	45 miles	Burrelton **	11 June 1956
Company	Caledonian	Coupar Angus	4 September 1967
		Ardler	11 June 1956
		Washington	November 1847
Stations closed	*Date*	Alyth Junction	4 September 1967
Ballathie	July 1868		
Cargill	11 June 1956		

Cargill Station.

* Closed stations on this line in Angus were Kirkinch, Eassie, Leason Hill, Glamis, Kirriemuir Junction, Forfar, Clocksbriggs, Guthrie, Glasterlaw, Farnell Road, Bridge of Dun, and Dubton.

** Known as Woodside and Burrelton until 1 September 1927.

Coupar Angus Station, April 1965.

This line was the Caledonian's main line from the south, linking Carlisle, Stirling, Perth and Aberdeen. Opened in 1848, it started at Stanley Junction north of Perth. This was where the Highland line to Inverness began and is still in use today. The line ran through the area called Strathmore and was fed by numerous lines coming in from the north and south. By the early 1960s the line was being used by some of the most powerful locomotives owned by British Railways, and as the only intermediate stations left were at Coupar Angus, Alyth Junction, Forfar and Bridge of Dun it was possible for the Glasgow to Aberdeen expresses to attain some very high speeds. When the line closed these services were diverted from Perth to Dundee and onwards up the east coast line to Aberdeen. A freight service to Forfar lasted until 1979 and today the Brechin Railway runs from the original Brechin Station to Bridge of Dun Station, providing a passenger services during the summer months.

A class 3F ex-Caledonian 0-6-0, no. 57581, at Alyth Junction with a railtour special, June 1962.

Closed passenger stations on lines still open to passenger services

Line/Service	Greenhill Upper Junction–Inverness *		
Kinbuck	11 June 1956	Strathord	13 April 1931
Greenloaning	11 June 1956	Stanley	11 June 1956
Carsbreck **	c.1935	Murthly	3 May 1965
Blackford	11 June 1956	Rohallion	October 1864
Auchterarder	11 June 1956	Dalguise	3 May 1956
Dunning	11 June 1956	Guay	3 August 1959
Forteviot	11 June 1956	Ballinluig	3 May 1965
Forgandenny	11 June 1956	Killiecrankie	3 May 1965
Perth Glasgow Road	May 1860	Black Island Platform ***	11 April 1959
Muirton Halt ***	21 November 1959	Struan	3 May 1965
Luncarty	18 June 1951	Dalnaspidal	3 May 1965

Kinbuck Station.

* Closed stations on this line in Stirlingshire were Plean, Bannockburn, and Bridge of Allan. Closed stations in Inverness-shire were Kincraig, Tomatin, Moy, Daviot, and Culloden Moor.

** Previously known as Royal Curling Pond Platform and used for Bonspiel curling matches.

*** Unadvertised platforms.

Greenloaning Station.

Auchterarder Station.

Dunning Station.

Forteviot Station.

The staff – and passengers – of Strathord Station.

Stanley Station.

The Tay Viaduct at Dalguise.

Ballinluig Station.

No. 126, 'Loch Tummel', entering Ballinluig Station.

Killiecrankie Station.